Casey

by Iain Gray

Lang**Syne**

PUBLISHING

WRITING *to* REMEMBER

WRITING *to* REMEMBER

79 Main Street, Newtongrange,
Midlothian EH22 4NA
Tel: 0131 344 0414   Fax: 0845 075 6085
E-mail: info@lang-syne.co.uk
www.langsyneshop.co.uk

Design by Dorothy Meikle
Printed by Printwell Ltd
© Lang Syne Publishers Ltd 2017

ISBN 978-1-85217-245-9

Casey

MOTTO:
By various fortunes
(and) Through many difficulties.

CREST:
A hand issuing from a cloud, lifting a Garb.

NAME variations include:
Ó Cathasaigh *(Gaelic)*
O'Casey
MacCathasaigh

Chapter one:
Origins of Irish surnames

**According to an old saying, there are two types of Irish –
those who actually are Irish and those who wish they were.**

This sentiment is only one example of the allure that the
high romance and drama of the proud nation's history holds
for thousands of people scattered across the world today.

It's a sad fact, however, that the vast majority of Irish
surnames are found far beyond Irish shores, rather than on
the Emerald Isle itself.

The population stood at around eight million souls in
1841, but today it stands at fewer than six million.

This is mainly a tragic consequence of the potato
famine, also known as the Great Hunger, which devastated
Ireland between 1845 and 1849.

The Irish peasantry had become almost wholly reliant
for basic sustenance on the potato, first introduced from the
Americas in the seventeenth century.

When the crop was hit by a blight, at least 800,000
people starved to death while an estimated two million
others were forced to seek a new life far from their native
shores – particularly in America, Canada, and Australia.

The effects of the potato blight continued until about
1851, by which time a firm pattern of emigration had
become established.

Ireland's loss, however, was to the gain of the countries in which the immigrants settled, contributing enormously, as their descendants do today, to the well being of the nations in which their forefathers settled.

But those who were forced through dire circumstance to establish a new life in foreign parts never forgot their roots, or the proud heritage and traditions of the land that gave them birth.

Nor do their descendants.

It is a heritage that is inextricably bound up in the colourful variety of Irish names themselves – and the origin and history of these names forms an integral part of the vibrant drama that is the nation's history, one of both glorious fortune and tragic misfortune.

This history is well documented, and one of the most important and fascinating of the earliest sources are *The Annals of the Four Masters*, compiled between 1632 and 1636 by four friars at the Franciscan Monastery in County Donegal.

Compiled from earlier sources, and purporting to go back to the Biblical Deluge, much of the material takes in the mythological origins and history of Ireland and the Irish.

This includes tales of successive waves of invaders and settlers such as the Fomorians, the Partholonians, the Nemedians, the Fir Bolgs, the Tuatha De Danann, and the Laigain.

Of particular interest are the *Milesian Genealogies*,

because the majority of Irish clans today claim a descent from either Heremon, Ir, or Heber – three of the sons of Milesius, a king of what is now modern day Spain.

These sons invaded Ireland in the second millennium B.C, apparently in fulfilment of a mysterious prophecy received by their father.

This Milesian lineage is said to have ruled Ireland for nearly 3,000 years, until the island came under the sway of England's King Henry II in 1171 following what is known as the Cambro-Norman invasion.

This is an important date not only in Irish history in general, but for the effect the invasion subsequently had for Irish surnames.

'Cambro' comes from the Welsh, and 'Cambro-Norman' describes those Welsh knights of Norman origin who invaded Ireland.

But they were invaders who stayed, inter-marrying with the native Irish population and founding their own proud dynasties that bore Cambro-Norman names such as Archer, Barbour, Brannagh, Fitzgerald, Fitzgibbon, Fleming, Joyce, Plunkett, and Walsh – to name only a few.

These 'Cambro-Norman' surnames that still flourish throughout the world today form one of the three main categories in which Irish names can be placed – those of Gaelic-Irish, Cambro-Norman, and Anglo-Irish.

Previous to the Cambro-Norman invasion of the twelfth century, and throughout the earlier invasions and settlement of those wild bands of sea rovers known as the Vikings in the eighth and ninth centuries, the population of the island was relatively small, and it was normal for a person to be identified through the use of only a forename.

But as population gradually increased and there were many more people with the same forename, surnames were adopted to distinguish one person, or one community, from another.

Individuals identified themselves with their own particular tribe, or 'tuath', and this tribe – that also became known as a clann, or clan – took its name from some distinguished ancestor who had founded the clan.

The Gaelic-Irish form of the name Kelly, for example, is Ó Ceallaigh, or O'Kelly, indicating descent from an original 'Ceallaigh', with the 'O' denoting 'grandson of.' The name was later anglicised to Kelly.

The prefix 'Mac' or 'Mc', meanwhile, as with the clans of the Scottish Highlands, denotes 'son of.'

Although the Irish clans had much in common with their Scottish counterparts, one important difference lies in what are known as 'septs', or branches, of the clan.

Septs of Scottish clans were groups who often bore an entirely different name from the clan name but were under the clan's protection.

In Ireland, septs were groups that shared the same name and who could be found scattered throughout the four provinces of Ulster, Leinster, Munster, and Connacht.

The 'golden age' of the Gaelic-Irish clans, infused as their veins were with the blood of Celts, pre-dates the Viking invasions of the eighth and ninth centuries and the Norman invasion of the twelfth century, and the sacred heart of the country was the Hill of Tara, near the River Boyne, in County Meath.

Known in Gaelic as 'Teamhar na Rí', or Hill of Kings, it was the royal seat of the 'Ard Rí Éireann', or High King of Ireland, to whom the petty kings, or chieftains, from the island's provinces were ultimately subordinate.

It was on the Hill of Tara, beside a stone pillar known as the Irish 'Lia Fáil', or Stone of Destiny, that the High Kings were inaugurated and, according to legend, this stone would emit a piercing screech that could be heard all over Ireland when touched by the hand of the rightful king.

The Hill of Tara is today one of the island's main tourist attractions.

Opposition to English rule over Ireland, established in the wake of the Cambro-Norman invasion, broke out frequently and the harsh solution adopted by the powerful forces of the Crown was to forcibly evict the native Irish from their lands.

These lands were then granted to Protestant colonists, or 'planters', from Britain.

Many of these colonists, ironically, came from Scotland and were the descendants of the original 'Scotti', or 'Scots', who gave their name to Scotland after migrating there in the fifth century A.D., from the north of Ireland.

Colonisation entailed harsh penal laws being imposed on the majority of the native Irish population, stripping them practically of all of their rights.

The Crown's main bastion in Ireland was Dublin and its environs, known as the Pale, and it was the dispossessed peasantry who lived outside this Pale, desperately striving to eke out a meagre living.

It was this that gave rise to the modern-day expression of someone or something being 'beyond the pale'.

Attempts were made to stamp out all aspects of the ancient Gaelic-Irish culture, to the extent that even to bear a Gaelic-Irish name was to invite discrimination.

This is why many Gaelic-Irish names were anglicised with, for example, and noted above, Ó Ceallaigh, or O'Kelly, being anglicised to Kelly.

Succeeding centuries have seen strong revivals of Gaelic-Irish consciousness, however, and this has led to many families reverting back to the original form of their name, while the language itself is frequently found on the fluent tongues of an estimated 90,000 to 145,000 of the island's population.

Ireland's turbulent history of religious and political strife is one that lasted well into the twentieth century, a landmark century that saw the partition of the island into the twenty-six counties of the independent Republic of

Ireland, or Eire, and the six counties of Northern Ireland, or Ulster.

Dublin, originally founded by Vikings, is now a vibrant and truly cosmopolitan city while the proud city of Belfast is one of the jewels in the crown of Ulster.

It was Saint Patrick who first brought the light of Christianity to Ireland in the fifth century A.D.

Interpretations of this Christian message have varied over the centuries, often leading to bitter sectarian conflict – but the many intricately sculpted Celtic Crosses found all over the island are symbolic of a unity that crosses the sectarian divide.

It is an image that fuses the 'old gods' of the Celts with Christianity.

All the signs from the early years of this new millennium indicate that sectarian strife may soon become a thing of the past – with the Irish and their many kinsfolk across the world, be they Protestant or Catholic, finding common purpose in the rich tapestry of their shared heritage.

Chapter two:

The vigilant warriors

The name stems from the Irish 'cathasach', indicating watchful, or vigilant, in war – and it would be difficult to find a more apt description for the generations of Caseys who played a formative role at key points in Ireland's turbulent history.

The Gaelic form of the proud surname Casey, or O'Casey, is Ó Cathasaigh and different septs of the family flourished in widely scattered locations throughout the land – including the modern-day counties of Kerry and Tipperary, Mayo, Dublin, Limerick, Cork and Fermanagh.

But what they and their descendants of today have in common is a truly illustrious pedigree that can be traced back to no less than three of the sons of the legendary King Milesius of Spain.

It is a complex and tangled genealogy, but its roots go back to when Milesius planned to invade Ireland in fulfilment of a mysterious Druidic prophecy.

Milesius died before he could launch his invasion across the sea to Ireland, but eight sons who included Amergin, Hebor, Ir, and Heremon undertook the task.

Five sons, including Ir, were killed in battle against the Tuatha De Danann shortly after battling their way from the shoreline to the soil of Ireland.

This was soil, however, that Ir's offspring and the offspring of his brothers Heber and Heremon were destined to hold for centuries as warrior kings.

According to the Milesian genealogies, Heremon and Heber began to rule the land they had conquered from about 1699 B.C.

Both Amergin and Heber were killed by Heremon in quarrels over territory, but the descendants of Ir, Heber, and Heremon thrived to found some of Ireland's greatest dynastic families.

The Caseys can trace a descent back to Heremon and, through marriage, to Heber, while a sept of Caseys was founded in present-day Westmeath by descendants of Ir.

The marriage that united the race of Heber and Heremon came about when Ciann, a son of the second century A.D. warrior king of Munster, Olliol Olum, married Sabia, a daughter of the legendary Conn of the Hundred Battles.

Caseys ruled as Lords of Saithne, in present day Co. Dublin, while another sept had a fiefdom centred on Liscannon, in present day Co. Limerick.

This sept had the added distinction of a kinship with the mighty Dalcassian confederation of clans of which the warrior king Brian Boru became leader.

It was Brian Borun who achieved a stunning victory over the Ostmen, or Vikings, at the battle of Clontarf on Good Friday of 1014, only to be killed in the immediate aftermath of the battle.

He had managed to achieve a temporary unity of sorts over the numerous squabbling petty chieftains and had been declared Ard Rí, or High King of Ireland.

But this unity was short-lived and it was not long before rival clans were battling among one another for supremacy.

This lack of unity was to prove to have disastrous consequences not only for the Gaelic order in general, but also for individual families such as the Caseys in particular, who were members of that ancient and glorious order.

By 1156 the most powerful of the Irish chieftains was Muirchertach MacLochlainn, king of the powerful O'Neills.

The equally powerful Rory O'Connor, king of the province of Connacht, opposed him but he increased his power and influence by allying himself with Dermot MacMurrough, king of Leinster.

MacLochlainn and MacMurrough were aware that the main key to the kingdom of Ireland was the thriving trading port of Dublin that had been established by invading Vikings, or Ostmen, in 852 A.D.

Dublin was taken by the combined forces of the Leinster and Connacht kings, but when MacLochlainn died the Dubliners rose up in revolt and overthrew the unpopular MacMurrough.

A triumphant Rory O'Connor entered Dublin and was later inaugurated Ard Rí, but the proud Dermott MacMurrough was not one to humbly accept defeat.

He appealed for help from England's Henry II in

unseating O'Connor, an act that was to radically affect the future course of Ireland's fortunes.

The English monarch agreed to help MacMurrough, but distanced himself from direct action by delegating his Norman subjects in Wales with the task.

These ambitious and battle-hardened barons and knights had first settled in Wales following the Norman Conquest of England in 1066 and, with an eye on rich booty, plunder, and lands, were only too eager to obey their sovereign's wishes and furnish aid to MacMurrough.

MacMurrough crossed the Irish Sea to Bristol, where he rallied powerful barons such as Robert Fitzstephen, Maurice Fitzgerald, and Hugh de Lacy to his cause, along with Gilbert de Clare, Earl of Pembroke.

The Normans invaded, and their onslaught on the forces of Rory O'Connor and his allies was so disciplined and fierce that by 1171 they had re-captured Dublin and other strategically important territories.

It was now that a nervous Henry II began to take cold feet over the venture, realising that he may have created a rival in the form of a separate Norman kingdom in Ireland.

Accordingly, he landed on the island, near Waterford, at the head of a large army in October of 1171 with the aim of curbing the power of his Cambro-Norman barons.

Protracted war between the king and the barons was averted, however, when they submitted to the royal will, promising homage and allegiance in return for holding the territories they had conquered in the king's name.

To the victors go the spoils, and one of the many beneficiaries of the Cambro-Norman invasion was Hugh de Lacy, who was granted vast territories previously held by the Caseys – including the territory of Saithne, near Dublin.

An Anglo-Norman invasion of the blighted land followed closely on the iron-shod heels of the Cambro-Norman invasion, with the power of the English Crown consolidated in Dublin.

There were now actually three separate Irelands.

There were the territories of the privileged and powerful Norman barons such as the de Lacys and their retainers, the Ireland of the disaffected Gaelic-Irish who held lands unoccupied by the Normans, and the Pale – comprised of Dublin itself and a substantial area of its environs ruled over by an English elite.

It was a recipe for disaster – with not only dispossessed Gaelic families such as the Caseys smarting under many grievances, but also a growing resentment on the part of many of the original invaders themselves over the increasing interference in their affairs by the English Crown.

Chapter three:

Rebels and writers

While some original Gaelic Irish families such as the Caseys would seek an accommodation of sorts with the English Crown and, in the case of some, would flourish as respected servants of the Crown, others found themselves drawn into insurrection and rebellion.

In the Civil War that exploded in the seventeenth century, Caseys were to be found on opposite sides of the religious, political, and military divides.

It was in 1641 that landowners rebelled against the English Crown's policy of settling, or 'planting' loyal Protestants on Irish land.

This policy had started during the reign from 1491 to 1547 of Henry VIII, whose Reformation effectively outlawed the established Roman Catholic faith throughout his dominions.

In the insurrection that exploded in 1641, at least 2,000 Protestant settlers were massacred, while thousands more were stripped of their belongings and driven from their lands to seek refuge where they could.

England had its own distractions with the Civil War that culminated in the execution of Charles I in 1649, and from 1641 to 1649 Ireland was ruled by a rebel group known as the Irish Catholic Confederation, or the Confederation of Kilkenny.

Among their number was Michael Casey, and he was to suffer dearly for his rebel stance.

Terrible as the atrocities against the Protestant settlers had been, subsequent accounts became greatly exaggerated, serving to fuel a burning desire on the part of Protestants for revenge against the rebels.

Tragically for Ireland, this revenge became directed not only against the rebels, but the native Irish such as the Caseys.

Following the execution of Charles I, and the consolidation of the power of England's Oliver Cromwell, the time was ripe was revenge.

Cromwell descended on Ireland at the head of a 20,000-strong army that landed at Ringford, near Dublin, in August of 1649.

He had three main aims: to quash all forms of rebellion, to 'remove' all Catholic landowners who had taken part in the rebellion, and to convert the native Irish to the Protestant faith.

An early warning of the terrors that were in store for the native Irish came when the northeastern town of Drogheda was stormed and taken in September and between 2,000 and 4,000 of its inhabitants killed.

The defenders of Drogheda's St. Peter's Church, who had refused to surrender, were burned to death as they huddled for refuge in the steeple and the church was deliberately torched.

A similar fate awaited Wexford, on the southeast coast, when at least 1500 of its inhabitants were slaughtered, including 200 defenceless women, despite their pathetic pleas for mercy.

Cromwell soon held the benighted land in a grip of iron, allowing him to implement what amounted to a policy of ethnic cleansing.

His troopers were given free rein to hunt down and kill priests, while rebel estates were confiscated, including those of Michael Casey.

An estimated 11 million acres of land were confiscated and the dispossessed native Irish banished to Connacht and Co. Clare.

An edict was issued stating that any native Irish found east of the River Shannon after May 1, 1654 faced either summary execution or transportation to the West Indies.

Charles Casey, meanwhile, who had taken no part in the Catholic Confederation, was rewarded with lands in Co. Cork that had been forfeited from rebels.

The island again exploded in a fury of discontent during the Rising of 1798, an ultimately abortive attempt to restore Irish freedom and independence.

In common with earlier rebellions, Caseys were found on opposite sides.

The roots of the Rising of 1798 are complex, but in essence it was sparked off by a fusion of sectarian and agrarian unrest and a desire for political reform that had been shaped by the French revolutionary slogan of 'liberty, equality, and fraternity.'

A movement had come into existence that embraced middle-class intellectuals and the oppressed peasantry, and if this loosely bound movement could be said to have had a leader, it was Wolfe Tone, a Protestant from Kildare and leading light of a radical republican movement known as the United Irishmen.

Despite attempts by the British government to concede a degree of agrarian and political reform, it was a case of far too little and much too late, and by 1795 the United Irishmen, through Wolfe Tone, were receiving help from France – Britain's enemy.

A French invasion fleet was despatched to Ireland in December of 1796, but it was scattered by storms off Bantry Bay.

Two years later, in the summer of 1798, rebellion broke out on the island, centred mainly in Co. Wexford.

The rebels achieved victory over the forces of the British Crown and militia known as yeomanry at the battle of Oulart Hill, followed by another victory at the battle of Three Rocks, but the peasant army was no match for the 20,000 troops or so that descended on Wexford.

Defeat followed at the battle of Vinegar Hill on 21 June,

followed by another decisive defeat at Kilcumney Hill five days later.

Although the Rising had proved abortive, it would act as a source of inspiration for succeeding generations of proud Irish nationalists and socialists – not least Seán O'Casey, born John Casey in 1880 and arguably one of the most famous Irishman to have born the name of 'Casey' in all its varied forms.

The great dramatist and memoirist certainly lived through interesting times until his death in 1964.

It was in the year of his birth in Dublin that James Parnell was elected chairman of the Irish Parliamentary Party, only a year after the foundation of the Irish National Land League.

By the time he was aged 18, the United Irish League had been founded, while a seminal moment in the life of this committed nationalist and socialist came when he was aged 36 in the form of the abortive 1916 Easter Rising in his hometown of Dublin.

Ireland did not become a Republic until 1949, by which time O'Casey had firmly established his reputation as a trenchant observer of his life and times and as a literary genius.

Forced through family circumstance to leave school at the age of 18 and working in a variety of jobs, O'Casey was aged 26 when he joined the Gaelic League and embarked on a study of the Irish language.

It may also have been during this period that he changed his name from 'John Casey' to the rather more Gaelic-sounding 'Seán O'Casey.'

A further expression of his nationalism was that he learned to play the Irish pipes, while he also joined the Irish Republican Brotherhood and became involved in attempts to improve the dire lot of Dublin's vast army of unskilled labourers.

His life took a martial turn in March 1914 when he became the general secretary of the Irish Citizen Army, only to resign from the post a few weeks later.

It is from this period onwards that O'Casey appears to have dedicated himself to the life of a writer – but it was a life infused with his deeply held nationalistic sentiments.

His play *The Shadow of a Gunman*, was performed in Dublin's famed Abbey Theatre in 1923, later followed by *Juno and the Paycock* and *The Plough and the Stars*.

The *Shadow of the Gunman*, although met with great critical acclaim, was highly controversial for its time, dealing as it did with the terrible events of the Irish Civil War, while *The Plough and the Stars* was set around the equally traumatic events of the Easter Rising.

O'Casey's dramatic depiction of the events of the Easter Rising was in fact so controversial that some sections of his audiences rioted – mistakingly believing that the playwright had written it from an anti-nationist stance.

O'Casey enjoyed success in the world of film,

particularly through the Hollywood director Alfred Hitchcock's adaptation of *Juno and the Paycock*.

Smarting under some of the criticism that was directed towards some of his plays, particularly *The Plough and the Stars* and his play *The Silver Tassie*, O'Casey eventually quit Irish shores to settle in England.

It was in this unlikely English setting that the ardent Irish nationalist went on to produce other great works, including *Within the Gates*, *The Stars Turn Red*, the 1949 *Cock-a-Doodle-Dandy*, and his six-volume *Autobiography*, before his death in Torquay in 1964.

Chapter four:

On the world stage

While Seán O'Casey excelled in the world of literature, his son Breon O'Casey, born in 1928, is the artist best known for his association with the Cornwall-based St. Ives school of painters and sculptors.

Also in the world of art, **Gerard Casey**, born in Kilkenny in 1960, is also a noted contemporary artist.

While not recognised as empire builders, at least two Caseys have achieved everlasting fame as city builders.

Born in Argentina in 1847 of Irish parents, the enterprising **Eduardo Casey** was aged 33 when he was able to buy 1,700 square miles of land in the province of Santa Fe and found what is now the flourishing city of Venado Tuerto.

According to tradition, the city is named after a one-eyed deer that would alert Casey and fellow early settlers to attacks by local and understandably warlike indigenous inhabitants of the area.

Casey was also instrumental in founding the town of Pigue, in Argentina's Saavedra region.

The equally enterprising and daring **Zadock Casey**, born in 1797, was responsible for the foundation in 1817 of the American city of Mount Vernon, in Illinois – while Casey Creek, a tributary of the state's Big Muddy River, is named after him.

Not only an entrepreneur but a politician, he also served in the Illinois State Senate.

On a musical note, **Al Casey** was the American jazz guitarist born in Louisville, Kentucky in 1915 who performed with jazz greats such as Fats Waller, Billie Holiday, and Frank Newton.

Composer of the hit *Buck Jumpin*, performed by Waller, he was still playing while aged into his late '80s; he died in 2005.

Another famed **Al Casey** was the rockabilly guitarist who was born in Long Beach, California, in 1936, and died in 2006, while **Kenneth Casey**, born in 1899, was the child actor and later author and composer responsible for the lyrics for the classic song *Sweet Georgia Brown*.

Born in Co. Waterford in 1959, **Karan Casey** is the Irish folk singer and jazz singer now based in the U.S.A., while **Natale Casey**, born in Lancashire in 1980, is the English actress who enjoyed musical success at the tender age of three with the song *Chick Chick Chicken*.

Better known as K.C. **Harry Wayne Casey**, born in Opa-Locka, Florida, in 1951, is the American musician best known for his group K.C. and the Sunshine Band. Producer of a string of hits for other artists, he is of mixed Italian-American and Irish-American roots.

From playing football with the San Francisco 49ers and the Los Angeles Rams, **Bernie Casey**, born in Wyco, West

Virginia, in 1939, turned to acting and has since appeared in films such as *Guns of the Magnificent Seven* in addition to an appearance on *Star Trek: Deep Space Nine*.

Born in Stockton-on-Tees in 1972, **Daniel Casey** is the actor who has appeared in a number of British television drama productions including *Midsomer Murders*, while also in the world of television drama **Ben Casey** was the title of a highly popular American medical drama that ran from 1961 to 1966 with Vince Edwards as Dr. Ben Casey.

In the highly competitive world of sport, **Don Casey** is the former American professional and collegiate basketball coach, while **Dwane Casey**, born in 1957 in Morganfield, Kentucky, is the former collegiate player who for a time was lead coach of the Minnesota Timberwolves.

Born in 1927, **Ron Casey** was the noted Australian Rules football administrator and commentator who died in 2000, while in the world of golf **Paul Casey**, born in Cheltenham in 1977 is the English player who in 2006 became the only player in the history of the Ryder Cup to win a foursome match with a hole-in-one.

Considered to have had one of the fastest serves in the world, **Ray Casey**, born in San Francisco in 1900 and who died in 1986, was a famed tennis player and coach.

In the world of books, **John Casey**, born in Worcester, Massachusetts in 1939, is the best-selling American writer who won the prestigious National Book Award in 1989 for his novel *Spartina*.

A number of Caseys have shown talent in the field of civil engineering, and no less so than **Thomas Lincoln Casey**, who was born at Sackets Harbor, New York, in 1831.

During the American Civil War, as Chief of Engineers for the United States Army Corps, he was responsible for the building of several military fortifications including the Maine coastal fortifications and Fort Knox, on the Penobscot River.

After the war he was responsible for the Office of Public Buildings and Grounds for the District of Columbia – and it was in this capacity that he built the State, War, and Navy Department building that is now the Eisenhower Executive Office Building.

He was also responsible for the completion of the magnificent Washington Monument and at the time of his death in 1896 had been working on the Library of Congress building.

His father, **Silas Casey**, born in East Greenwich, Rhode Island, in 1807, also served as a United States Army officer during the American Civil war and wrote the three-volume *System of Infantry Tactics*.

Another talented engineer who also served as a soldier was Hugh Casey, better known as **Pat Casey**, born in Brooklyn, New York in 1898 and who died in 1981.

A Major General in the U.S. Army during the Second World War, he served as chief engineer to General Douglas MacArthur and was responsible for the extremely arduous task of constructing airstrips and roads and other vital military infrastructure in the inhospitable terrain of New Guinea.

His son, **Hugh Casey**, also served his country. Camp Casey, in South Korea, was named after him following his death during the Korean War.

Both father and son are buried in Washington's Arlington National Cemetery.

Also on the field of battle, **George Casey**, born in 1922, was the U.S. Army General who was in command of the 1st Cavalry Division during the Vietnam War.

He was killed in a helicopter crash in 1970, but his son, **George Casey Jnr.**, has carried on the military tradition. Born in 1948, he is now a General in the U.S. Army and was appointed Chief of Staff of the United States Army in 2007.

In the clandestine and often murky world of international espionage **William J. Casey**, born in Queens, New York in 1913 and who died in 1987, served as director of the Central Intelligence Agency (C.I.A.) from 1981 to 1987.

Born in Firies, Co. Kerry in 1927, **Dr. Eamon Casey** is the controversial Roman Catholic Bishop Emeritus of Galway and Kilmacduagh who received decidedly unwanted attention in 1992 when it was revealed that he had had an affair with an American divorcee and that they had a son.

He had also been at the centre of controversy eight years earlier when, because of his opposition to U.S. foreign policy, he refused to meet President Ronald Reagan when he visited Galway.

A rather less controversial religious figure was Bernard Francis Casey, who took the name of **Father Solanus Casey** after being ordained into the Roman Catholic priesthood in 1904.

Born in Oak Grove, Wisconsin, in 1870, he died in Detroit in 1957 and was buried in the St. Bonaventure Monastery; his remains were later exhumed, however, and placed in the Father Solanus Casey Center, attached to the monastery, because of his fame as a healer and prophet.

Pope John Paul II declared in 1995 that Father Casey was 'Venerable' – one of the steps on the path to eventual sainthood – and the Father Solanus Casey Center is visited by growing numbers of pilgrims every year.

Also in the realms of healing, **Anne Casey**, is the New Zealand-born nurse, now resident in Britain, who is responsible for the **Casey Model of Nursing**, and who was made a Fellow of the Royal College of Nursing for her services to paediatric nursing.

Albert Casey, who was born in 1920 and who died in 2004, was the colourful publisher of the *Los Angeles Times* and former United States Postmaster General who once famously asserted that any business should consist of 'a person to make the stuff, a person to sell the stuff, a bean counter to keep score, and a boss.'

He also coined the **Casey's Law** aphorism that 'if something can go right, it should.'

Key dates in Ireland's history from the first settlers to the formation of the Irish Republic:

circa 7000 B.C.	Arrival and settlement of Stone Age people.
circa 3000 B.C.	Arrival of settlers of New Stone Age period.
circa 600 B.C.	First arrival of the Celts.
200 A.D.	Establishment of Hill of Tara, Co. Meath, as seat of the High Kings.
circa 432 A.D.	Christian mission of St. Patrick.
800-920 A.D.	Invasion and subsequent settlement of Vikings.
1002 A.D.	Brian Boru recognised as High King.
1014	Brian Boru killed at battle of Clontarf.
1169-1170	Cambro-Norman invasion of the island.
1171	Henry II claims Ireland for the English Crown.
1366	Statutes of Kilkenny ban marriage between native Irish and English.
1529-1536	England's Henry VIII embarks on religious Reformation.
1536	Earl of Kildare rebels against the Crown.
1541	Henry VIII declared King of Ireland.
1558	Accession to English throne of Elizabeth I.
1565	Battle of Affane.
1569-1573	First Desmond Rebellion.
1579-1583	Second Desmond Rebellion.
1594-1603	Nine Years War.
1606	Plantation' of Scottish and English settlers.

1607	Flight of the Earls.
1632-1636	Annals of the Four Masters compiled.
1641	Rebellion over policy of plantation and other grievances.
1649	Beginning of Cromwellian conquest.
1688	Flight into exile in France of Catholic Stuart monarch James II as Protestant Prince William of Orange invited to take throne of England along with his wife, Mary.
1689	William and Mary enthroned as joint monarchs; siege of Derry.
1690	Jacobite forces of James defeated by William at battle of the Boyne (July) and Dublin taken.
1691	Athlone taken by William; Jacobite defeats follow at Aughrim, Galway, and Limerick; conflict ends with Treaty of Limerick (October) and Irish officers allowed to leave for France.
1695	Penal laws introduced to restrict rights of Catholics; banishment of Catholic clergy.
1704	Laws introduced constricting rights of Catholics in landholding and public office.
1728	Franchise removed from Catholics.
1791	Foundation of United Irishmen republican movement.
1796	French invasion force lands in Bantry Bay.
1798	Defeat of Rising in Wexford and death of United Irishmen leaders Wolfe Tone and Lord Edward Fitzgerald.

1800	Act of Union between England and Ireland.
1803	Dublin Rising under Robert Emmet.
1829	Catholics allowed to sit in Parliament.
1845-1849	The Great Hunger: thousands starve to death as potato crop fails and thousands more emigrate.
1856	Phoenix Society founded.
1858	Irish Republican Brotherhood established.
1873	Foundation of Home Rule League.
1893	Foundation of Gaelic League.
1904	Foundation of Irish Reform Association.
1913	Dublin strikes and lockout.
1916	Easter Rising in Dublin and proclamation of an Irish Republic.
1917	Irish Parliament formed after Sinn Fein election victory.
1919-1921	War between Irish Republican Army and British Army.
1922	Irish Free State founded, while six northern counties remain part of United Kingdom as Northern Ireland, or Ulster; civil war up until 1923 between rival republican groups.
1949	Foundation of Irish Republic after all remaining constitutional links with Britain are severed.